Christian F Gardner

Local Taxation

An Essay on the Injustice, Inequalities, and Anomalies of the Present

Poor-Rate Assessment, and the Incidence of other local Burdens in

England and Wales

Christian F Gardner

Local Taxation

An Essay on the Injustice, Inequalities, and Anomalies of the Present Poor-Rate Assessment, and the Incidence of other local Burdens in England and Wales

ISBN/EAN: 9783337329648

Printed in Europe, USA, Canada, Australia, Japan

Cover: Foto ©Suzi / pixelio.de

More available books at **www.hansebooks.com**

Prize Essay.

LOCAL TAXATION:

An Essay

ON THE INJUSTICE, INEQUALITIES, AND ANOMALIES OF THE PRESENT POOR-RATE ASSESSMENT,

AND

THE INCIDENCE OF OTHER LOCAL BURDENS IN ENGLAND AND WALES.

BY

CHRISTIAN F. GARDNER, B.A., Cantab.,

STOKE DAMEREL, DEVON.

TO WHICH WAS AWARDED THE PRIZE OFFERED BY THE LOCAL TAXATION COMMITTEE.

"This is not the cause of faction, or of party, or of any individual, but the common interest of every man in Britain."—Junius.

PUBLISHED BY THE LOCAL TAXATION COMMITTEE,

At the office of "Chamber of Agriculture Journal,"

21, ARUNDEL STREET, STRAND, W.

Price 2d. each (post free 3d.), or 16s. per 100.

F. BENTLEY AND CO., PRINTERS, SHOE LANE, FLEET STREET.

CONTENTS.

———◆———

CHAPTER I.

CHAPTER II.

CHAPTER III.

CHAPTER IV.

CHAPTER V.

CHAPTER VI.

LIST OF TABLES.

LOCAL TAXATION:

AN ESSAY.

————◆————

CHAPTER I.

A COMMITTEE of the National Assembly, appointed to inquire into the state of the poor in France, described our Poor-law system as " *La plaie politique la plus dévorante de l'Angleterre* " *; and at that time there were many Englishmen who re-echoed this opinion. In these days few would venture to assert so odious a calumny; and it is now almost universally acknowledged that it is the duty of a civilized country to make a legal provision for its poor. In England the legislature has given to the poor an absolute right to relief.

The duty of providing for the impotent poor was first recog- nized in the year 1388 †; but vagabondage and mendicity were treated with the utmost rigour. In the times of the early Tudors the feudal power of the nobility had been undermined by the civil wars between the rival houses of York and Lancaster; and the abolition by Henry VII. of the system of " maintenance " had compelled bands of lawless men, hitherto supported by the nobles in idleness, to seek their own living.

The suppression of the religious houses by Henry VIII., and the consequent extinction of the charity which they had been accustomed to exercise, removed a great source of relief to the poor, and the country swarmed from end to end with able bodied mendicants. The sole idea of English rulers appears to have

———

* The most wasting sore in the political system of England.

† 12 Ric. II. c. 7.

been to treat pauperism as a crime. Whipping, branding, and even death were the penalties inflicted upon the sturdy beggar under the statutes of Henry VII. and Henry VIII. These enactments defeated themselves by their own severity. People did not like to enforce them. In the reign of Edward VI. (A.D. 1551) a milder act was passed. It appointed collectors of alms, who were " gently to ask of every man and woman at church that they of their charity should give weekly to the relief of the poor "; and if any, who were able to give, refused to do so, the bishop was to send for the recusant, and use " charitable ways and means." This voluntary system of poor relief does not appear to have been effectual. It remained for the wise and sagacious statesmen, who guided the councils of Queen Elizabeth, to devise measures for the management of the poor, which admirably answered the ends of humanity and utilised the immense labour power of the country, which, whilst unemployed, was a curse instead of a blessing. In the year 1563, an Act* was passed empowering justices of the peace to tax at their discretion any one who refused to give voluntarily towards the maintenance of the poor ; and in default to send him to jail. At length, in 1601,† the Act was framed and passed which has formed the foundation of the Poor-Law system to the present time. And, as in the following pages frequent reference will be made to this statute, it is here quoted :—

" Be it enacted by the authority of this present Parliament, that the churchwardens of every parish, and four, three, or two substantial householders there, as shall be thought meet, having respect to the proportion and greatness of the same parish and parishes, to be nominated yearly in Easter week, or within one month after Easter, under the hand and seal of two or more justices of the peace in the same county, whereof one to be of the quorum, dwelling in or near the same parish, or division where the same parish doth lie, shall be called overseers of the poor of the same parish ; and they, or the greater part of them, shall take order from time to time, by and with the consent of two or more such justices of peace as is aforesaid, for setting to work the children of all such whose parents shall not, by the said churchwardens and over-

* 5 Eliz. c. 3.   † 43 Eliz. c. 2.

seers, or the greater part of them, be thought able to keep
and maintain their children; and also for setting to work all
such persons, married or unmarried, having no means to
maintain them, and use no ordinary and daily trade of life
to get their living by; and also to raise weekly or otherwise
(by taxation of every inhabitant, parson, vicar, and other, *Who are to be taxed for*
and of every occupier of lands, houses, tithes impropriate, *the relief of*
propriations of tithes, coal-mines or saleable underwoods, in *the poor.*
the said parish, in such competent sum and sums of money
as they shall think fit), a convenient stock of flax, hemp, *A convenient*
wool, thread, iron, and other ware and stuff, to set the poor *stock to be provided to set*
on work; and also competent sums of money for and towards *the poor on*
the necessary relief of the lame, impotent, old, blind, and *work.*
such other among them being poor, and not able to work;
and also for the putting out of such children to be appren-
tices, to be gathered out of the same parish, *according to the*
ability of the same parish, and to do and execute all other
things, as well for the disposing of the said stock, as otherwise concerning the premises, as to them shall seem convenient."

Can any unprejudiced mind doubt that the spirit of this Act *The Act*
intended every inhabitant to contribute according to the means *intended every inhabitant to*
which he possessed? It is impossible to suppose that the framers *be taxed*
of it intended to depart from what had been the custom clearly *his ability.*
established by preceding statutes, that universal contribution was
expected according to every man's ability. By the Act of Edward VI.
the contribution was voluntary; and a moral pressure only could
be brought to bear against a non-contributor. By the Acts of the
5th and 43rd of Elizabeth the contribution was made compulsory
and the tax was legally recoverable.

The Statute expressly mentions both "inhabitants" *and*
" occupiers " which would seem intended to include both residents
and non-residents; so that none should escape. Inhabitants, as
such, were to be rated according to their ability, and occupiers of
property, even if non-resident, were to be liable in respect of that
property. This interpretation would make trades, professions,
and personal property rateable as well as real property; and the
Act was so interpreted by the Committee of the House of Lords

appointed in 1850* to inquire into the Parochial Assessment system. The 6th resolution of the Committee states :—

" That the relief of the poor is a national object, towards which *every description of property* ought justly to be called upon to contribute, and that the Act of 43rd Elizabeth, c. 2, contemplated such contribution according to the ability of every inhabitant."

This intention was carried out to some extent in the 18th century, for in the last legal decision (R. *v.* Lumsdaine), we find Chief Justice Littledale saying,

" Hitherto, rates upon inhabitants in respect of personal property, have been in practice confined to stock-in-trade and shipping."

But the assessment of stock-in-trade has since been abandoned as impracticable, it being nearly always impossible to ascertain its rateable value ; and moreover, the owner was subjected to the vexatious and inquisitorial visits of the overseer. The great inconvenience caused by this state of things, led to the passing of the Exemption Act† in 1840, which is still periodically renewed. This Act provided that no inhabitant should be rated for his stock-in-trade or other personal property ; and as Sir George Cornewall Lewis said in his evidence before the Committee of the House of Lords in 1850, it suspended " the rateability of inhabitants in respect of the ability of the parish." We may therefore consider the word " inhabitant " as practically struck out of the Act of Elizabeth. The ratepayer is now charged in his character of occupier only ; except in those comparatively few cases (to be hereafter noticed),‡ in which the rates are paid by the owner, under the " Poor-Rate Assessment and Collection Act, 1869." It may be remarked, however, that, as the Exemption Act is passed for limited periods, and renewed from time to time, the Government does not deny the principle that personal property should contribute to the Poor-rates.

The Poor-rates, as established by the 43rd of Elizabeth, were originally intended solely for the relief of the poor : but, as the system affords a convenient basis for collection, various other rates, all of which are national in their objects, have been at various times engrafted on the Poor-rate; and at the present time, under the name of Poor-rates, the occupiers of real property are taxed for many objects totally unconnected with the relief of the poor. This will be seen from the following Table, * which is compiled from the 21st Annual Report of the Poor-Law Board. Appendix C., Nos. 23 and 24.

Various other rates have been engrafted on the Poor-rates.

* See Table I.

TABLE I.

Year ending Lady-day, 1868.

Total amount levied for Poor-rate £11,054,513

Deduct Expenditure for

(1) Purposes *connected* with the Relief of the Poor :
   viz., Costs of proceedings at Law or in Equity £28,832

(2) Purposes *unconnected* with the Relief of the Poor :
   viz., County, Hundred, Borough, or Police-rate £2,456,578
   Highway Boards 614,893
   Constables' expenses, and Costs of proceedings before Justices 36,281
   Fees to Clergymen and Registrars, Outlay for Register, Offices, Books and Forms 73,826
   Vaccination Fees and Expenses 50,987
   Expenses in respect of Municipal or Parliamentary Registration, and Cost of Jury Lists 39,199
                                                    ———————
                                                    3,271,764

(3) Purposes *partly connected* and *partly unconnected* with the Relief of the Poor :
   viz., Payments under Parochial Assessments Act, and Union Assessments Committee Acts 49,734
   Expended for other purposes, such as, Burial Boards, Baths and Washhouses, Fire Brigade, Salaries of Collectors, etc. 532,204
                                                    ———————
                                                    581,938
                                                    ———————
                                                    3,882,534

Balance 7,590,309

Deduct the difference between Levy and Expenditure 92,250

Actual Expenditure for Relief to the Poor £7,498,059

From this Table it may be observed that one-third of the whole amount levied as Poor-rates is expended for purposes unconnected with the Relief of the Poor.

But, besides these various rates which are all included under the title of Poor-rates, there are others, all of which are charged upon the same kind of property, and which, with Poor-rate levy, make up the Local Taxation of England and Wales.

A summary is given below in Table II.

TABLE II.

Local Taxation in England and Wales falling on Real Property, 1867-68.*

	£
1. Amount levied under the name of Poor-rates (see Table I.)	11,054,513
2. Amount levied for County, Hundred, Borough, and Police-rates, in cases where these are not paid out of Poor-rates	307,232
3. Highway-rate, where separately levied	916,779
4. Church-rates	217,038
5. Lighting and Watching-rates...........................	76,978
6. Improvement Commissioners...........................	445,431
7. General District Rates under Public Health Acts	1,736,247
Ditto† ditto ...	60,443
8. Rates under Courts of Commissioners of Sewers, including Drainage and Embankment-rates ...	695,810
Ditto† ditto ...	13,261
9. Rates of other kinds, including a sum of £981,140 levied in the Metropolitan District for General and Lighting Rates	1,203,397
	£16,727,174

N.B. It will at once be seen that items 1 and 2 in this Table are *national* in their objects, the remainder being *local*. This portion of the subject is treated fully at pp. 55, etc.

It should be here noted, that there is a discrepancy of

* Local Taxation Returns, 497, and † 497—I.

£6,989 between the total in Table II. and that given by the
Local Taxation Returns (497—I). It is thus accounted for:
The amount of Poor-rate levied in 1868, as shown in the
Twenty-first Annual Report of the Poor Law Board, was furnished
by the Clerks of the Guardians, and is £11,054,513, being
£6,989 less than the sum shown in the Local Taxation Returns,
the particulars of which were furnished by the Overseers of each
separate parish, and amount to £11,061,502. In Tables I. and
II., the amount of the Poor-rate levy is taken from the Report
of the Poor Law Board.

Let it be kept in mind, that the whole of this enormous
amount of Local Taxation, given in Table II., is levied upon real
property only; and, in order to show more clearly how heavily
such property is taxed, Table III. gives the average rate in the
pound, and the average rate per cent. paid by the property
assessed to Local Taxation.

TABLE III.

Local Taxation, 1867-68.

Gross estimated Rental of Property assessed* £118,334,081
Rateable value of ditto* 100,612,734
Total Local Taxation† 16,727,174
Amount of Poor-rate levy‡ 11,054,513
Amount expended in actual relief to the Poor‡   7,498,059

	On Gross Estimated Rental.		On Rateable Value.	
	s.	*d.*	*s.*	*d.*
Average Rate in the Pound of Total Local Taxation .	2	9·9	3	3·9
„ Poor-rate Levy.........	1	10·4	2	2·4
„ Actual relief to the Poor	1	3·2	1	5·9

* Local Taxation Returns, 497.   † Table II.   ‡ Table I.

	On Gross Estimated Rental.	On Rateable Value.
	£	£
Average Rate per cent. of Total Local Taxation .	14⅓	16⅝
„ Poor-rate Levy	9⅚	11
„ Actual relief to the Poor	6⅓	7¹¹⁄₁₄

In order rightly to understand the subject of Local Taxation, it is necessary to have a clear conception of what is implied by the terms, "gross estimated rental" and "rateable value."

The "gross estimated rental" is "the rent at which the hereditament might reasonably be expected to let from year to year, free from all usual tenant's rates and taxes, and tithe commutation rent-charge, if any."* That is to say, it is the rent, not including rates and taxes, which a tenant would be willing to give annually; or, in other words, a tenant pays rates and taxes in addition to the "gross estimated rental."

The "rateable value" is "an estimate of the net annual value of the several 'hereditaments, rated thereunto' (i.e. relief to the poor); that is to say, of the rent at which the same might reasonably be expected to let, from year to year, free from all usual tenant's rates, and taxes, and tithe commutation rent-charge, if any; and deducting therefrom the probable annual average cost of the repairs, insurance, and other expenses, if any, necessary to maintain them in a state to command such rent."†

In other words, if the average annual cost of repairs, insurance, etc., be deducted from the "gross estimated rental," the remainder will be the "rateable value," or "net annual value," upon which the rates are to be levied.

From this it will be seen, that a yearly tenancy is taken as the standard for estimating the rateable value of any hereditament.

An example will make the matter clear. Let it be supposed that a person is willing to pay £100 annually for a house. He

Marginal note: Explanation of "Gross Estimated Rental" and "Rateable Value."

Marginal note: Example.

* 25 & 26 Vic., c 103, s. 15, Union Assessment Committee Act.
† 6 & 7 William IV., c. 96, s. 1, Parochial Assessment Act.

finds that the rates and taxes amount to £20 per annum. He therefore offers to pay the landlord £80 a year rent. This sum is the "gross estimated rental." But the whole of it will not find its way into the landlord's pocket, for in a yearly tenancy it is customary for the landlord to pay for insurance, repairs, etc. The charges for these, on such a house as we are supposing, would average about £12 per annum. The "net annual value" to the landlord is therefore £68, and this is the "rateable value" of the house, on which sum the tenant would be rated.

It will at once be perceived that, although the principle, on which the "gross estimated rental" and the "rateable value" are to be determined, is clearly laid down here, yet in applying this principle to practice, there is no guarantee for uniformity of valuation. The valuations, upon which the Poor-rates are

Inequalities arising from the different systems of valuation. charged, are made by assessment committees and overseers, whilst the magistrates make another valuation upon which the County-rates are levied. These last are made on a uniform system throughout each county; though different counties frequently differ in their systems. But with regard to Poor-rates, each assessment committee may have its own system of determining what is a correct estimate of the gross rental; and that being settled, may also have its own system for determining what deductions should be allowed, so as to arrive at the "rateable" or "net annual value." The confusion hence arising causes much injustice; and the want of a uniform system of accurate valuation gives rise to many inequalities and anomalies. It is not easy to show the inequalities of the various valuations for the "gross rental;" but in column (6) of Table IV. is given the difference per cent. between the "gross rental" and the "rateable value" in twenty-eight unions in England and Wales, this difference being the sum allowed per cent. for the cost of insurance, repairs, and other expenses necessary to maintain the property valued in a state to command the gross rental. These deductions vary from 6⅔* per cent. for the Union of St. George's, Hanover Square, to 35⅔ per cent. for Great Yarmouth. Can there be an instance of greater inequality than this? In Manchester, the ratepayers are allowed to deduct 17 per cent. from the gross rental: but in Salford, a town adjoining Manchester, they may only deduct 10⅓ per cent. At Great Yarmouth they

* See Column (6), Table IV.

may deduct 35¾ per cent., whilst at Norwich, in the same county, only 16½ per cent. deduction is allowed.

The writer of an article in the *Edinburgh Review* says* : —

" We believe that the people of this country have but little reason to complain of the taxation levied by the State. It is equally imposed, it is cheaply collected, it is honestly spent. But of the enormous sums levied under the form of rates and Local Taxation the very reverse must be said.

*   *   *   *   *   *   *

This is really the oppressive and unjust portion of our public burdens. It is assessed with excessive inequality and injustice by parochial boards, subject to no general control, and deaf to remonstrance ; it is collected by non-official persons, and it is spent nobody knows how—at least in the metropolis, and in many other towns of the empire."

Now that Table IV. is before us, it may be well to observe another great inequality which exists between the different Unions in the amounts paid in the pound for the actual relief of the poor. Thus a reference to column 11 will show that, whilst the City of London and St. George's, Hanover Square, pay only 7*d.* and 8*d.* in the pound respectively, Bethnal Green pays 3*s.* 11*d.*, King's Lynn 4*s.* 4½*d.*, Great Yarmouth 4*s.* 7*d.* *Inequalities in different Unions in the amounts paid in the £.*

Even with respect to the present system of Local Taxation, what seems first to be required is a common basis of valuation throughout the country. But equity would also insist upon the income arising from personal property, trades, and professions being made liable to this taxation ; and then the impost should be equally distributed over the whole country, so that the wealthy. as at the West end of London, should bear their share of the poorer, as at the East end.

† *Edinburgh Review,* January, 1869.

TABLE IV.

Unions arranged in Union County Order. (1)	Area in Statute Acres. (2)	Population in 1861. (3)	PAROCHIAL YEAR 1867—68. Gross estimated Rental. (4)	Rateable Value. (5)	Difference per cent. between Cols. (4) and (5). (6)	Total Local Taxation. (7)	Rate in £ of Col. (7) on Col. (5). (8)	Poor Rates levied. (9)	Expended in Relief to Poor. (10)	Rate in £ of Col. (10) on Col. (5). (11)
Metropolitan.			£	£	£	£	s. d.	£	£	s. d.
St. George's, Hanover Squ.	1,161	87,771	970,996	905,812	6⅔	117,554	2 8	78,971	30,104	0 8
Hampstead	2,252	19,106	270,288	204,772	21⅕	38,669	4 7¼	14,957	6,610	0 7¾
City of London	434	45,555	2,263,146	1,836,135	19	294,979	3 3¼	63,707	52,962	0 7
Bethnal Green	760	105,101	329,946	220,906	33	85,166	7 6½	55,919	43,356	3 11
St. George's in the East	243	48,891	227,318	181,119	20⅓	71,819	7 9¼	43,654	31,463	3 5¾
Stepney	576	56,572	302,721	246,756	18½	80,110	6 6	55,738	44,223	3 7
Country.										
Brighton		77,693	456,701	386,513	15⅘	107,980	5 7	77,422	49,434	2 6½
Portsea Island		94,828	284,487	243,014	14½	81,937	6 9	50,328	46,297	3 9½
Southampton		43,414	207,311	163,550	21	57,419	7 0¼	29,257	23,146	2 10
Colchester		23,809	91,582	74,647	18¼	20,311	5 5¼	16,374	12,877	3 5¼
Great Yarmouth		30,338	97,188	62,484	35¾	21,871	7 0	14,886	14,337	4 7
Norwich		74,440	245,147	204,736	16½	72,583	7 1	32,726	30,595	2 11¼
King's Lynn		16,701	61,891	44,960	27⅓	16,206	7 2½	11,346	9,862	4 4½
Salisbury		9,039	30,048	24,045	20	9,425	7 10	5,390	4,735	3 11¼
Exeter		33,738	157,669	125,027	20⅗	35,591	5 8¼	15,948	10,729	1 8½
Plymouth		62,599	189,308	156,637	17	53,492	6 10	31,951	23,347	2 11
Stoke Damerel		50,440	95,559	72,680	24	23,219	6 4¾	13,210	13,890	3 9¾
Stoke-upon-Trent		71,308	246,024	206,700	12	50,642	4 10¾	28,361	21,221	2 0½
Wolverhampton		111,033	383,665	307,893	19⅔	78,092	5 0¾	47,289	29,467	1 3
Birmingham		212,621	915,604	734,986	19⅔	111,528	3 0½	111,528	80,078	2 2
Coventry		41,647	135,000	114,447	15¼	25,173	4 4½	15,406	12,057	2 0
Nottingham		74,693	298,987	263,397	12	74,143	5 7½	36,016	25,787	1 11½
Liverpool		269,742	2,005,205	1,804,677	10	392,773	4 4¼	156,717	155,451	1 8½
Salford		105,335	484,554	434,370	10⅓	112,537	5 2¼	60,341	30,172	1 3¾
Manchester		185,410	1,171,857	973,542	17	199,054	4 1	136,304	86,057	1 9
Bradford		106,218	572,341	489,019	14½	122,745	5 0¼	40,512	21,748	0 10½
Sheffield		128,673	554,738	414,332	25⅓	130,945	6 3¾	46,176	45,661	2 1¼
Swansea		51,260	199,059	180,316	9½	59,606	6 7¼	29,328	22,290	2 5¾

Metropolitan—See Appendix D., No. 46, Twenty-first Annual Report of Poor Law Board. Column (4) is taken from Tocal Taxation Returns, 497. (See Summary of Unions.)

Country—Columns (3), (4), (5), (7), (8), are taken from Local Taxation Returns, 497; Columns (9) and (10) from Appendix C., No. 24, Twenty-first Annual Report of Poor Law Board; Columns (6) and (11) are computed from these data.

CHAPTER II.

THE property which is at present subject to Local Taxation, may be divided into three branches :—

(I.) Land, including Tithe rent-charge.

(II.) Houses, including Shops, Factories, Warehouses, etc.

(III.) Railways, Canals, Coal-mines, Quarries, Gas and Water-works.

(I.) The rates upon land are collected from the occupier, who is assessed upon the "net annual value," or "rateable value," of his holding. Now, land is either rented and occupied by a tenant, or the owner is himself the occupier. The law holds the occupier responsible for the due payment of the rates, and in default distrains his goods.

It is often asserted, that the whole of the rates are ultimately paid by the owner, because an intending tenant will calculate what are the outgoings in the form of rates, taxes, etc., before he offers a rent to the landlord. It is said, therefore, that rates are a deduction from rent, and that any redistribution, which would, to a certain extent, relieve the property now chargeable, would benefit the landlord only. In theory this is quite correct. Outgoings are calculated upon the average of past years ; and, if the rates were a fixed charge, it might justly be said that the landlord pays them : but in practice there are various disturbing influences. Experience shows, that rates are a steadily increasing tax. How then would this affect a tenant holding a lease ? It must be seen at once that the total increase of the rates, since he became the occupier, has come out of his own pocket. The annual amount levied for Poor-rates has increased during the past ten years by nearly three millions. In 1858* the amount levied was £8,188,880, in 1868 it was £11,054,513. Intending tenants could not have taken this increase into consideration, when esti-

* Twenty-first Annual Report of Poor-Law Board. Appendix C., No. 29.

mating what rent they could afford to give. Sir George Cornewall
Lewis,* in his evidence before the Committee of the House of
Lords in 1850, gave, as his opinion, that

> " Any sudden or unexpected increase of parochial expen-
> diture would, until the contract was readjusted, fall entirely
> upon the tenant."

The tenant gets no compensation for this increase ; and " a
very high authority" has informed Mr. Dudley Baxter,†

> " That there is such a competition for land and houses,
> that, even where property is relet, the *old* rather than the
> *new rates* are supposed to belong to the landlord, and all the
> *fresh outgoings* to the tenant. You may fairly say that all
> the increase of rates within the last twenty-five years has
> fallen upon the occupier."

It is clear, then, that no inconsiderable amount of the present
Local Taxation falls on the tenant.

The effect of the competition for land on intending tenants.
But it is said that, in case the rates were reduced by a redistribution, the great competition for lands and houses would
influence intending tenants to offer a rent increased by just so
much as the Local Taxation was diminished, and so landlords would
ultimately gain the amount. This argument would apply to any
other cause which might make his farm more profitable to the
tenant, such as the opening of a railway in the neighbourhood,
thereby affording a better market for agricultural produce. In
this case would competition compel the tenant, at the expiration
of his lease, either to give the whole benefit of the increased
profit to his landlord, or to resign his farm to another who would
be ready to do so ? Those who reply in the affirmative forget
that there is a competition amongst landlords for good tenants.
The system of rack-rents is not carried out fully in practice.
Farms are not always let to the highest bidder; but, when a
landlord has a good and improving tenant on his land, he is
desirous of retaining him, and therefore would be willing to allow
him a fair portion of the increased advantages. The rent would,
indeed, be increased : but landlord and tenant would each have a

* Lords' Committee on Parochial Assessments, 1860. Q. 32.
† "Taxation of the United Kingdom." Ch. xii., p. 61.

share in the profits. And just so it is with regard to the reduction of local burdens. It is true, that, if in isolated cases the local rates were reduced, competition would cause an intending occupier to offer as rent what he would before have paid in rent and taxes together: but, if the rates were generally reduced throughout the country, it does not follow that competition would enable the owner to monopolize the whole benefit. This would imply that there were as many good and desirable farmers out of business, as, at the time of reduction, there were occupiers. It is then for the mutual interest of owner and occupier that the rates should be reduced.

Mr. Dudley Baxter is of opinion that the " average inci-dence of rates is *three-fourths on the landlord* and *one-fourth on the tenant.*"[*]

And this calculation has been adopted in the following pages: but, as the rates are increasing every year, and it has been shown that the increase falls on the tenant, it would appear that the proportion of incidence on the tenant is also annually increasing.

But if the landlord and tenant would be gainers by a more general arrangement of the Local Taxation, it stands to reason that those who occupy and farm their own estates would be benefited in a much greater degree, for they would reap the whole advan-tage of any reduction. More particularly would this affect the yeomen and small freeholders, upon whom the present system presses very heavily and unjustly. Suppose the case of a pea-sant, who has saved sufficient money to buy an acre of land, and is desirous of building a cottage on his plot of ground. Having laid out his money in the land, he borrows enough to build his cottage. For this loan he would pay interest, and not only so, but he would have to pay rates on the whole property, the rate-able value of which would be taken upon both the original pur-chase and the outlay in building, whilst only the former would really belong to him. The lender, meanwhile, who has thus invested his money, would enjoy the interest without paying a single farthing towards the rates.

The case of the beneficed clergy also deserves attention. The clergyman is rated in the same manner as other occupiers on his

Incidence on freeholders and yeomen.

Example.

Incidence on the beneficed clergy.

---

[*] " Taxation of the United Kingdom." Ch. xii., p. 62.

glebe and glebe-house. He is also rated on the tithe rent-charge, from which the greater part of his income is usually drawn ; and, in addition to the heavy Local Taxation, he is expected to give liberally to voluntary charities.

In the following extract from the letter of "An Essex Rector,"* the position of the beneficed clergy is forcibly described :—

> " The clerical possessor of tithe rent-charge is not in the same position as the landlord of the soil. In almost all cases the clergyman, by his death, ceases to have any interest in the rent-charge. He cannot take it with him ; he cannot will it away ; a stranger succeeds him in the enjoyment of it, as unknown to him as his predecessor was; and therefore the living is not to him a property in the same sense that a landed estate is to a family with a succession of heirs, and therefore a living ought not to be rated as land.
>
> " Again, while it must be allowed that, since the passing of the Tithe Commutation Act, no incumbent obtains his real tenth of the income of a parish ; and worse still, no matter how the property improves and the population increases—and, consequently, the clergyman's work—his income does not increase in correspondence ; yet there are so many rates and taxes, never dreamt of at the time of the passing of the Commutation Act, now included in that monstrous charge called the Poor-rate, that the clergyman most improperly, if not unlawfully, is made to pay more than is right, and has no possibility of obtaining redress, so as to have equal taxation with his neighbours."

Effect of Local Taxation on the agricultural interest. Having considered the incidence of the local burdens upon the various classes of landholders, it will be instructive to observe what is the effect of this taxation upon the agricultural interest. No one will assert that the productive resources of land in England and Wales are now made the most of. There can be no doubt that a larger supply both of corn and meat might be obtained from the same area. There are thousands of acres, now lying almost useless, which would ultimately pay well for being **Example.** drained and brought under cultivation. Let it be supposed that

* Letter from "An Essex Rector."—"Times," Feb. 10, 1869.

there is a tract of land of this description, which would only just pay a fair remuneration for being cultivated, even if no rent were paid for it. The owner would be willing to give an active and enterprising tenant a lease of it at a nominal rent, on condition that he improved it. It would be necessary for the tenant to lay out capital. He would have to employ labour which was previously unemployed. This would tend to raise the rate of wages in that district, thereby lessening the call upon the Poor-rates. As the land improved, there would be a greater supply of food produced at home, thus obviating the necessity of importing so much from foreign lands. This would have the effect of cheapening agricultural produce, and the community at large would be benefited. But assessment committees have the power of increasing the rateable value of a farm, as the occupier invests his personal property in it. As soon, then, as it is perceived that the barren land is improving, the assessment committee will at once come down on the tenant; and, supposing he had invested £1000 of capital, he would probably be charged £16 or £17 for rates. It has been assumed above that the tenant would only just be remunerated for cultivating this land, if he held it at a nominal rent. The consequence is he will be losing £16 or £17 per annum on the £1000 he has invested. No one can be expected to be satisfied with this result, or to persevere in an unremunerative undertaking.

The present system of Local Taxation is therefore a direct discouragement to the investment of capital in agriculture; for it involves a heavy tax on outlays in improvements. It is calculated to diminish the demand for labour, and so to lower the rate of wages. It tends to cripple the productive power of the country, to necessitate the importation of food, which might be produced at home, and therefore to raise its price.*

Local Taxation a discouragement to the investment of capital in agriculture.

---

* Since the above was written, a letter from Norwich, under the signature "F. S. C.," has appeared in the "Chamber of Agriculture Journal." An extract is here given, in which the writer fully corroborates the argument given above:—

"Five years since, a farm in this neighbourhood was let to a tenant under the following conditions, namely, that for the first four years he should pay no rent; for the ten years next ensuing his rent was set at a sum approximately that of the adjoining farms in an average state. The condition of the farm at entry fully justified this.

"In the first four years the tenant's outlay upon improvements amounted to

The English farmer has to contend against great competition from foreign countries, where the climate is more favourable, and where land and labour are much cheaper than at home ; and it requires the greatest exertion to compete successfully. Agriculture used formerly to be encouraged by the imposition of heavy duties on the importation of foreign agricultural produce. Whilst this system of protection existed, by which agriculturists gained special benefits, it was only fair to others that they should bear special taxation ; but now that protection has been abolished by the adoption of free trade, wealth, as derived from other sources than real property, has increased to a marvellous extent ; and it is no longer just that those sources should remain exempt from Local Taxation.

In February, 1851, Mr. Disraeli stated that " owners and occupiers were more heavily weighted with taxation than any

about £3000. Now, let us mark what took place in the assessment of such a place. During the first four years, when, as I have said, the tenant paid no rent (with a view to prospective improvements), the assessment was made (properly; as I think) upon an assumed annual value, proportionate to its existing state during the twelve months next accruing; and this without reference to any statement made of the actual rent. The principle (otherwise applicable) of a valuation *in communibus assessis* was deemed inapplicable in this case.

" At the end of the fourth year (the valuation not having been changed), an appeal upon the part of the parish took place ; and, by order of the assessment committee, a regular survey was made. At that time, by the judicious outlay of a considerable capital, the farm had reached a pitch of culture considerably beyond that of most in the same parish, and upon the report of the valuers the assessment was considerably increased. Nevertheless, so unfair did it seem to the committee that such should be the incidence of the tax, that a special reference was taken upon one point, namely, whether, under the whole circumstances detailed, any abatement should be made to replace capital laid out. The fiat was against this.

" Surely it is idle to ask upon whom is the incidence of this tax—his landlord or himself.

" Nor can I leave such an instance without a further remark, addressed to those who (like myself) have the welfare of the agricultural labourer as well as the farmer at heart.

" Amongst them there are economists as well as philanthropic gentlemen, and the former, at all events, will comprehend this fact—that it is, and must be, the application of capital which determines the labourer's state. Without an increase of capital, no increase of wages can take place.

" One question let me ask. Does capital seek out an industry thus heavily taxed ? Invested in manufacture, would this man's £3000 have been liable to such a burden as this ? Would the per-centage derived have been less ?"— " Chamber of Agriculture Journal," Oct. 18th, 1869, p. 723.

other class, because taxation had been adjusted to their shoulders during the existence of an artificial system which insured them a good market for their productions, but which system was now removed; and he protested against flinging upon the land a disproportionate share of burdens, which, as they were raised for the behoof of the general public, ought to be equally and impartially distributed over the whole general public."

Both Sir Robert Peel and Earl (then Lord John) Russell pledged themselves that, when the policy of free trade should be adopted, it would be only just and right that it should be accompanied by a policy of fair taxation. This measure of justice and equity has never been carried out, and commerce and manufactures, by their exemption from Local Taxation, are, in fact, protected at the expense of agriculture. One result of this system may be seen in the annually diminishing number of small farms cultivated by their owners. The yeomanry of England bore a very important part in the early history of the country, but now, owing partly to the extensive use of machinery in agriculture, which a small farmer cannot afford, and partly to the great increase of burdens on land, the yeoman, being unable to earn reasonable profits, finds it advantageous to himself to sell his estate to some large proprietor in the neighbourhood, and invest the proceeds in a more lucrative business. Thus it happens that the small freehold farms are being continually absorbed. This fact is well worth the attention of those who advocate the system of peasant proprietors.

But it is often urged that the profits of a farmer are much greater than those of a fundholder, and, therefore, he ought to bear a larger amount of taxation. The profits of a farm should be such as to answer at least the following reasonable demands. *The profits of farming, compared with those of other occupations.*

1st. The interest at the ordinary rate on the capital invested in the farm.

2nd. The sum due as wages to the farmer for supervision; for if he were not the overseer of his own farm, he would have to pay a bailiff to superintend it for him. The farmer would probably do twice the work of a man who was hired.

3rd. The insurance against risk to live and dead stock.

If these last two items be deducted from a farmer's profits, it is very doubtful whether the remaining item, viz., the rate of interest on his invested capital, exceeds that which a fundholder receives for his investments, about which he has no risk and no trouble of superintendence. But, however this may be, it is certain that farming is not nearly so lucrative as many retail trades.

Rates upon houses, etc.

(II.) The greater part of rates upon houses, shops, factories, etc., falls upon the inhabitants of cities and towns, and, as in the case of land, are collected from the occupier on the "rateable value" of the house, except in the instances hereafter noted at page 27, *inf.* But the rent paid for houses differs in some points from that paid for land. The element of productiveness does not enter into the calculation of a tenant when he is determining what rent he will offer for a house. With regard to land this is one of the principal considerations. Again, if the house be one of a limited number, situated in the heart of a good neighbourhood, the competition for it will be so great, that the owner can demand almost what rent he pleases, without allowing any drawback for rates. In this case the occupier would pay the whole of the Local Taxation: but where there are a considerable number of houses, from which an intending occupier may choose, as in the suburbs of a town, he calculates the amount of the rates, and offers so much less rent: but, after he has made this agreement, any increase of local burdens will fall on him as it does on the tenant of land; and from dislike of changing his abode, or because he has become attached to the house, he will continue to pay these increased rates when he has to renew his lease.

*cidence on *ners and *cupiers of *vellings.

Mr. Dudley Baxter * considers "that on the average of house property, the incidence of rates, may be estimated at *two-thirds on the landlord, and one-third on the tenant,* where the rates are paid by the tenant; but that the landlord pays a larger proportion when they are compounded for by him.

"But in order to avoid any under-estimate of the pressure of taxation on the tenant," Mr. Dudley Baxter takes "the rates on houses as paid *half by the landlord and half by the tenant.*"

* " Taxation of the United Kingdom." Ch. xii. p. 66.

This calculation has been adopted in the following pages, and it is probably the more correct estimate of the two.

By the Poor Rate Assessment and Collection Act, 1869,* occupiers of tenements let for short terms, not exceeding three months, may deduct the Poor-rate paid by them from their rents, and no such occupier can be compelled to pay at one time, or within four weeks, a greater amount of the rate than would be due for one quarter of a year. The object of this is to ensure that the occupier shall not be required to pay, as Poor-rate, a sum which he cannot within a short period recoup himself by deduction from his rent. Here then the owner would pay the whole of the rates. Where the rateable value of any hereditament does not exceed twenty pounds, if situate in the Metropolis; or thirteen pounds if situate in any parish wholly or partly within the borough of Liverpool; or ten pounds if situate in any parish wholly or partly within the city of Manchester or the borough of Birmingham; or eight pounds if situate elsewhere, the owner may agree to pay the rate and be allowed a commission not exceeding twenty-five per cent. on the amount thereof. Here the owner will pay the greater part of the rates. It is also to be noted, that to entitle him to the commission he must pay whether the hereditament be occupied or not.

Business premises, factories, mills, etc., are frequently the property of the occupier; but their rateable value must be determined, as in other cases by considering what would be their " net annual value." This it is often very difficult to do, as probably there will be no similar premises near, and it will be impossible therefore to institute a comparison by which to measure the value. In all these the occupier may be making thousands a year profit, but he is only rated on the premises in which he dwells, and in which he carries on his business. The artisan employed at a factory would, according to Mr. Baxter's theory, pay about half † the amount levied on his dwelling, and there can be no doubt that, even though he may only have to pay 16s. 8d.‡ per annum, this is a very great hardship to a man who is earning only from £50 to £60 per annum,—a very much greater hardship than paying £100 per annum is to his employer, who is perhaps clearing

(marginal note:) Incidence on the owners and occupiers of business premises, factories, etc.

---

* 32 and 33 Vict., c. 41, s. 1—3. See Edition of the Act by H. Owen, Esq.
† See p. 26, *supra*.   ‡ See Table V., p. 33, *infra*.

£5000 per annum. Mr. Rathbone, the Member for Liverpool, speaking in the House of Commons on the 22nd of June last, is reported to have said,—

"The principal wealth of our large towns consisted of commercial, manufacturing, and trading interests; but, except incidentally, none of these interests contributed to the Poor-rate, and the more their wealth had increased the more they had escaped from anything like a legitimate amount of contribution to the support of the poor. They did not pay on their capital, because that capital, consisting mainly of personalty, was not subject to Local Taxation. Nor did they contribute in the towns on their domestic establishments, because now, the merchant, the banker, or the broker, instead of living on the spot where his business was conducted, resided out of town. The fact that men of the class to which he referred paid so insignificant an amount towards the relief of the poor had, he was convinced, a good deal to do with their withdrawal from a discharge of the duties of Poor Law guardian. A merchant, doing a large business in a moderately large office and warehouse, only paid rates for those premises, whatever might be the extent of his transactions. Merchants, who had made the calculation, informed him that the proportion of their income derived from trade on which they paid Poor-rate amounted to only from *one-half* to *two per cent.*, while the proportion of their income on which labourers, in the employment of those merchants, paid Poor-rates was 3¾ per cent. From this it appeared that the proportion, in which persons paid in large towns, was in almost inverse ratio to their wealth. Upon the class of small tradesmen the Poor-rate operated most oppressively, and with especial severity upon those who were in the humblest circumstances. It might be said that it was foolish for the mercantile community to be active in promoting a change of system; but the mercantile community were not foolish or shortsighted enough to believe that a system could be good, which transferred a considerable portion of the burden of taxation from their shoulders to those of the very poor."

In levying Income-tax for imperial purposes, incomes under

£100 per annum are exempted, and incomes between £100 and £200 per annum are allowed to deduct £60 before paying the tax; but the occupier of the smallest holding must pay local rates, and cases have been known of people coming upon the Poor-rates for relief who were actually at the time in debt to the overseers for arrears of rates, with which they had been charged, but which they had not been able to pay. It is not fair that those whose incomes but just remove them above the level of poverty, should be charged with the payment of rates for the relief of the poor.

The high rates levied upon houses tend to discourage the building and improvement of the smaller kind of dwellings, particularly those inhabited by the working classes. Capitalists will not lay out their money in building cottages, when they cannot get as good interest as may be obtained from other investments, in consequence of these local taxes. There is, therefore, a less demand for the labour, both skilled and unskilled, of those who would be employed in house-building; and worse than this, there is not sufficient decent accommodation provided either in towns or villages for the working population. Dwellings are over-crowded, whole families frequently living together in one room. Moreover, the population of towns is rapidly increasing. At the census of 1861, it was found that there were nearly 11 millions residing in 781 towns, and little more than 9 millions in the villages and country districts; that is, 55 per cent. reside in towns, and 45 per cent. in other parts of England and Wales. It has been computed that, at the close of the present century, at least 64 per cent., or nearly two-thirds of the whole population will be found in towns. If there is not room enough at present, what can be expected with an increase of town population, but an increase of disease and vice, and the miserable demoralization of all who are brought up under such influences. "S. G. O.,"* writing to the "Times," goes straight to the point when he ascribes the great increase of pauperism and crime to the want of decent habitations for the labouring classes. He gives a vivid picture of the homes in which poverty and crime go hand in hand.

Effect of Local Taxation on the dwellings of the working classes.

"When to the idea of the man we try to attach the idea

* Letter from "S. G. O."—"Times," Jan. 25, 1869.

of his home, we at once domicile him in some wretched, narrow, ill-drained, filthy locality, where, not himself ' the compound householder,' he is yet with his wife, or the woman so called, a portion of a compound household, consisting of as many of the same class, or worse than himself, as the dirty rooms, attics, cellars, can contain; men, women, and children are there, all breathing a foul atmosphere, fed on coarse and often most foul food; stale fish, washed down with adulterated spirits, a very common diet. As to decency, it is not merely non-existent, but all around would stifle in the birth any attempt at it. Religion! why, blasphemy is there, not the outbreak of anger into impious language; it is in such places one of the chief elements of language which go to make up ordinary intercourse. How in such a scene can any one teach children to love God and reverence the law? There have been, doubtless, many glorious instances where imported adult piety, compelled to dwell thus, has yet survived; but how is it possible to conceive that the native —the bred and born there—can have one wholesome idea as to soul or body? In so rank a soil, in such an atmosphere, could industry, honesty, chastity, sobriety survive? Its trading community are in character with the general population; all that is sold is of the worst, all that is bought is at its last—where it is not the fruit of robbery.

      *   *   *   *   *   *

"Is it not the case, that all the while we are deploring the increase of paupers, and execrating the increasing breed of daring criminals, we do keep up immense breeding areas, stocked to the overflow with men, women, and children, who, compared with all other life, are bred to a vermin life? We cry out for more Poor-law officials, more stringent dealing with paupers. We clamour for more activity in the police, and police power, to catch the robber when he leaves the locality, where there is nothing worth stealing, for the watch and plate regions, and yet we either cannot, or will not, go to the root of the evil, and try to diminish this dangerous breed of beings by letting the light of ordinary civilization into their scene of dwelling.

" We spend in a few years a few million pounds on public buildings and 'embankments,' on all manner of construction, which may, while it proves our enterprise, tend to exalt the outward character of the Metropolis; a drive after dark along our great shop thoroughfares affords a wonderfully illuminated spectacle of all that art can effect to fashion every valuable material of this earth into articles of use or *luxe :* a wonderful picture it all is of the demands of civilization, in aid of all its invented necessities. And yet, beneath all this, often very close to it—certainly, ever within a mile or two of it—are hundreds of thousands of human beings, living the life of utter decivilization ; nay, worse than this, the progress of other class improvement, the claims of wealth, have so occupied the ground, that year by year the dwelling space for all labouring men becomes further contracted ; and those who are industrious hate pauperism—who are honest, and would rear their children so, can only find their dwellings as they may, at any cost to body and soul, in these nurseries of guilt.

" The Church has tried churches and chapels. Dissent has put forth all its missionary energy ; philanthropy has worked with a will and a zeal above all praise . . . . . . Our great gaol and house of correction, penitentiary, and reformatory institutions, are already on a large scale, and yet there is ever a cry for more space for the treatment of criminals, for the rescue of penitents. To my mind, *so long as we shunt the dwelling question,* all this religious, and charitable, and legal apparatus, is only so much mill power to grind the grist of the crop we see growing—know must so grow, *so long as we submit the labouring classes to a pressure in the matter of home—which must drive them to such a home, that, bred without decency, they must grow up without shame.*

" It is my firm conviction that the condition of the classes who, as paupers and criminals, now excite so much anxiety, has yet to be made known in all the depth and breadth of its real danger to the nation—that there are beneath all the outward show of wealth increasing, luxury advancing, elements of danger to our whole social commonwealth, and that these are the result of our own wilful blindness to the causes which have begotten them. The real truth is, as yet we have been content to deal only with the effect of the degradation of our poor, doing this on no one well-considered principle. The true causes of that degradation have formed themes for much writing and declamation, but the ruling powers of the nation have hitherto avoided any effectual dealing with them."

The average rate in the pound of Local Taxation for England and Wales is shown in Table III.* to be 3s. 4d. approximately (3s. 3·9d.) ; and the ratio of the incidence has been found to be 4s. 2d. on towns, to 2s. 6d. on the rural districts ; the difference being principally due to rates in towns levied under the Public Health and Local Government Acts, and for Drainage, Sewerage, and Lighting, all of which are purely local objects; and therefore all inhabitants of towns ought to contribute according to their ability, as all reap the benefit.

The ability to contribute to be measured by income.
Now the ability of any one to contribute is best measured by his income. The opposite table gives the rate in the pound of Local Taxation on the incomes of various occupations of the community : and shows clearly the unequal incidence of Local Taxation in towns as well as rural districts; and that it is to the interest of dwellers in both to strive for a reform.

Observe here that although the manufacturers' income is equal to the landed proprietor's, the former pays but one-fourth the amount of Local Taxation imposed on the latter. And so, whilst the tradesman's income is double that of the yeoman, the former pays little more than a third of the rate paid by the latter.

Rates upon railways, etc.
(III.)　Railway property is of three kinds, viz. :—

Debenture bonds and stock.
Preference shares and stock.
Ordinary shares and stock.

Incidence on railway shareholders.
The debenture bonds and preference shares are not charged to the rates, so that the whole of rates on railways are paid by the ordinary shareholders. This has the effect of raising the cost of traffic both of persons and of things. It is, in fact, an indirect tax on locomotion. It is found that 62 per cent. of those who travel by railways are third-class passengers. These, then,

* See page 14, *supra.*

TABLE V.

Description of owner of income. (1)	Income per annum. (2)	Rateable value. (3)	Average rate in £ of rates on col. (3). (4)		Total amount of rates charged. (5)			Proportion paid by each owner in col. (1). (6)	Actual incidence of rates on owners in col. (1). (7)			Rate in the £ of col. (7) on col. (2) (8)	
	£	£	s.	d.	£	s.	d.		£	s.	d.	s.	d.
1. Landed Proprietor deriving an income of £5,000 from rents	(a) 5,422	4,500	2	6	563	0	0	$\frac{3}{4}$	422	0	0	1	6½
2. Manufacturer being the owner of his own premises	5,000	500	4	2	104	0	0	whole	104	0	0	0	5
3. Tenant Farmer	200	360	2	6	45	0	0	$\frac{1}{4}$	11	5	0	1	1½
4. Professional Man	500	60	4	2	12	10	0	$\frac{1}{2}$	6	5	0	0	3
5. Yeoman	(b) 150	90	2	6	11	5	0	whole	11	5	0	1	6
6. Tradesman..........................	300	40	4	2	8	6	0	$\frac{1}{2}$	4	3	0	0	3¼
7. Clerk	99	15	4	2	3	2	6	$\frac{1}{2}$	1	11	3	0	3¾
8. Artisan	60	8	4	2	1	13	4	$\frac{1}{2}$	0	16	8	0	3¼

(a).—If a landlord receives an income of £5,000 per annum from rents, and the total rates upon his property amount to £563, the incidence is £422 upon himself, because he receives so much less rent than he otherwise would, whilst £141 is paid by his tenants, *i.e.*, he pays three-fourths and his tenants one-fourth. Therefore, in calculating the rate in the pound on his income (column (8)) paid by the landlord himself, we must take £5,422 and not £5,000 as his income; because, if the rates were abolished, his income would be increased by £422. It must be remembered that the whole sum, £563, is collected from his tenants.

(b).—A yeoman is here supposed to farm land of which the gross annual rent would be £100. The income from this, calculated according to the Imperial Income-tax valuation would be £50 per annum; but as the land is the yeoman's own property, he has no rent to pay. His income is therefore £150 per annum.

who can least afford it most feel the pressure of rates on railways, for if the rates were diminished, as they might be by a redistribution, they would travel just so much the cheaper. In many of the canal acts there is a special clause stating in what manner the particular canal is to be rated; but the incidence of the rates is very much the same as in the case of railways. The rates are charged upon the shareholders, and the general public suffer. They are an indirect tax upon traffic.

Canals.

With regard to coal mines and quarries,* " the produce, for the right to enjoy which the rent is paid, is derived from the *sale* of the *corpus*, and not merely the use of it." Coal-mines are usually worked by companies, and the proprietor generally receives a stipulated portion of the gross returns as a consideration for the use and deterioration of his property. In agreeing what this portion or royalty shall be, the company of course take into consideration the rates they will have to pay; and any increase of the rates will fall upon them. The incidence of the rates may therefore be considered the same as in the case of land, partly on the occupiers or company who work the mine, and partly on the proprietor. There is no doubt also that the price of the coal and stone excavated is in some degree affected by the rates, so that here also the community would share the benefit if the rates were diminished by a re-arrangement.

Coal mines and quarries.

In the case of gas and waterworks the whole of the rates ultimately fall upon the consumer. As the rates increase the occupiers or proprietors of the works will increase the price of the gas or water.

Gas and waterworks.

* Penfold on Rating, p. 59 (5th Ed.).

CHAPTER III.

THE gross rental of the property on which the Local Taxation for England and Wales was raised in the year 1868 is estimated at £118,334,081* and the rateable value at £100,612,734. This property is for the most part the same as that which was assessed to Income-tax for Imperial purposes under Schedule A before the 5th of April, 1866. At that† date railways, canals, etc., were transferred to Schedule D. Their annual value for 1868 is estimated by Mr. Purdy at £29,041,932,‡ but Mr. Purdy has included a sum of £1,526,790, dividends on foreign securities, which, not being chargeable to the local rates, must be deducted, leaving £27,515,142.

The income charged to Local Taxation compared with the income of the country generally.

The latest return§ assigning the amounts of income charged to Income-tax under each Schedule is for the year 1867. Mr. Purdy gives the amount of income charged under Schedule A alone, for the year 1868; but, in order to make an impartial investigation of the incidence of the taxation, it will be necessary to know the amounts under the other Schedules. In the following calculations, therefore, the Income-tax returns for 1867 are taken.

The net annual value of real property, on which the Income-tax was collected, may be put thus:—

	£
Under Schedule A	100,546,389
Sum formerly charged under A, but since 1865 transferred to D, as profits	27,515,142
Total	£128,061,531

---

* See Table III., p. 14, *supra*.   † 29 Vict., c. 36.

‡ Journal of the Statistical Society, Vol. xxxii., pt. 3, pp. 309 and 324.

§ Twelfth Report of Commissioners of Inland Revenue. App., p. xiii.

The difference between this total and the rateable value of property assessed to Local Taxation is £27,448,797. This difference must not be attributed wholly to defective valuation on the part of assessment committees and overseers, because some real property under Schedule A, and some of that transferred to Schedule D, is exempt from local rates.

Now the total income of England and Wales, upon which the Income-tax was raised for the year 1867, amounted to £302,294,505,* and since the local rates are levied on £100,612,734 of income, it appears that the whole of the Local Taxation of the country is paid by less than *one-third* of the income which is chargeable to Income-tax for Imperial purposes. But the income shown under the Income-tax returns by no means represents the actual income. It is well-known that incomes under £100 per annum are not included in these returns. Incomes between £100 and £200 per annum are excused the tax on £60. Again, there are unreturned profits of trades and professions under Schedule D. Mr. Dudley Baxter puts the income of the manual labour classes at £254,729,000.† Table VI. gives the aggregate income of all classes in England and Wales approximately for the year 1867.

TABLE VI.

Approximate Income of all Classes in England and Wales, 1867.

Mr. Dudley Baxter, "National Income," p. 34.	(a) Income-tax† charged in 1867 on	£302,294,505
	The £60 per annum excused to incomes between £100 and £200 per annum‡...	10,000,000
	Incomes under £100 per annum, not charged to Income-tax and not derived from manual labour	60,000,000
	(b) Unreturned profits under Schedule D ...	49,075,712
	Income of Upper and Middle Classes ...	421,370,217
	Earnings of manual labour§	254,729,000
	Total..............	£676,099,217

* See Table VI.   † " National Income," p. 52.
‡ Twelfth Report Inland Revenue Commissioners, App. xiii.
§ " National Income," p. 52.

Note (a).—This amount differs from that given in the 12th Report of H.M.'s Commissioners of Inland Revenue, which is £316,676,079. The difference is accounted for by the fact that under Schedule B the rent paid by farmers is given as £28,763,148 ; but a farmer's profits chargeable with Income-tax are supposed to be half his rent. Hence the income of those assessed under Schedule B is £14,381,529.

(*b*).—The unreturned profits, or sum on which Income-tax was evaded under Schedule D, is estimated by H.M.'s Commissioners of Inland Revenue at £57,254,997,* the estimate being made for the United Kingdom. Now the income of England and Wales, assessed under Schedule D, is † six times the income of Scotland and Ireland together, under the same Schedule. Hence the unreturned profits may be taken as

£49,075,712 for England and Wales.

8,179,285 for Scotland and Ireland.

which is probably an under estimate for England and Wales.

This vast amount of fraud will be discussed hereafter,‡ when the consideration of the statistical part of the subject is ended.

The income, therefore, of all classes in England and Wales being £676,099,000 approximately, it appears that that which is subject to Local Taxation is considerably less than *one-sixth*—indeed, very little more than *one-seventh*—of the whole income of the country. This is a very great anomaly ; and a redistribution of the burden would seem to be urgently required by justice and equity, unless it can be shown that the property which bears it enjoys privileges which are denied to other kinds of property, or that other property is subject to taxation for objects from the support of which real property is exempt, and which might be placed as a set-off against the Local Taxation.

In order, then, to form an impartial judgment on this matter, it will be necessary to consider the system of taxation for Imperial purposes in connection with the existing system of Local Taxation, and to view the bearing of both upon the community generally. We shall omit from our calculations, as not germane to the subject, all such taxes as are ultimately paid indirectly by

The system of Imperial Taxation, in connection with the system of Local Taxation.

* Twelfth Report, p. 23.   † Twelfth Report, App., p. xiii.

‡ See page 41, *infra.*

the customer or consumer ; because the cost of them is added by
the merchant or vendor to the wholesale or retail price, merely
remarking here that the manual labour classes contribute their
share to this indirect taxation.   These taxes are Excise duties,
taxes on patents, bills of exchange and bankers' notes, newspapers,
patent medicines, gold and silver plate, and duties on cards.   The
assessed taxes, with the exception of house duty, are also omitted,
because they are voluntarily incurred by the taxpayer.

The Imperial Taxation of England and Wales (with the above
exception) is given in Table VII. for the year 1868.

TABLE VII.

Imperial Taxation.—1868.

(*a*) Stamps on Deeds and other Instruments	£1,405,000
Probates of Wills and Letters of Adminis-	
tration, etc.	1,382,000
Legacy and Succession Duties...........	2,445,000
(*b*) Receipts, Drafts, and other 1*d.* Inland	
Revenue Stamps	500,000
Marine Insurances	156,000
Licences and Certificates	98,000
Probate Court Fee Stamps	124,000
Admiralty Court Do.	11,000
Land Registry Do.	1,000
(*b*) Companies' Registration Fee Stamps ...	7,000
Common Law Court Fee Stamps	112,000
Land Tax	1,058,000
House Duty	1,003,000
Property and Income Tax	
Real Property 2,354,000	
From other Sources 2,845,000	
	5,199,000
Total..................	£13,501,000

Thus we have—

Imperial Taxation	13,501,000
Local Taxation*	16,727,000
Total Taxation, with the exceptions ⎰	£30,228,000
mentioned above .... ⎱	

* Table II., p. 13, *supra.*

Note (*a*). The stamps on deeds, etc., are taken from Mr. Purdy's paper in the "Journal of the Statistical Society," vol. xxxii., part iii., page 311.

(*b*). The Inland Revenue Stamps and Companies' Registration Fee Stamps are given for the United Kingdom in the 12th Report of Her Majesty's Commissioners of Inland Revenue, appendix, p. v. The figures in Table VII. are an estimate for England and Wales.

It may be observed here that none of this Imperial Taxation is paid by the manual labour classes. The whole of it is borne by the upper and middle classes, whose income is estimated at £421,370,000 in Table VI.

Now let us compare the amount of Imperial Taxation paid by income from real property, with the amount paid by income from other sources.

TABLE VIII.

Imperial Taxation in England and Wales falling on real property in 1867-68, or thereabouts, according to returns in possession of Her Majesty's Commissioners of Inland Revenue.*

Property and Income Tax, 1867	2,354,000
Land Tax, 1868	1,058,000
House Duty, 1868.............................	1,003,000
Succession Duty, 1868	608,000
(*a*) Stamps on Deeds and other Instruments, 1868	1,405,000
(*b*) Probate of Wills and Letters of Administration	
(*c*) Legacy Duty on Real Property, directed by Will to be sold	
(*d*) Probate Court Fees	
(*e*) Land Registry Fees	
Approximate Total	£6,428,000

Note (*a*).—Stamps on sales, conveyances, leases, mortgages, are included in this sum, but it is impossible to distinguish accurately, what portion is incident on real property.

(*b*).—The stamp duties on Wills and Letters of Administration, some of which will be paid on leaseholds for years, and there-

* Mr. Purdy, Journal of the Statistical Society, vol. xxxii., pt. iii.; p. 331.

fore indirectly from real property are excluded from the above Table.

(c).—By the Succession Duty Act (16 & 17 Victoria, c. 51, s. 29), real property directed by will to be sold is chargeable, like personal property, with legacy duty ; except where, under the said Act, it is chargeable with duty as a succession. This is also excluded.

(d) and (e).—Probate Court Fees and Land Registry Fees have been omitted.

It is more than probable that these exclusions (b), (c), (d), (e), will balance the excess under the head of stamps on deeds (a).

To find the amount of Imperial Taxation borne by other than real property, deduct the total in Table VIII. from the first total in Table VII. thus:—

Total Imperial Taxation...........................	£13,501,000
Ditto ditto ditto borne by real property	6,428,000
Total Imperial Taxation borne by other than real property...................................	£7,073,000

It has* before been estimated that three-fourths of the local taxes are paid by the owner, and one-fourth by the occupier. In the case of other real property, one-half is paid by the owner and one-half by the occupier. And Mr. Purdy states that, in 1865, *landed* property, including tithe rent-charge, bore 35·3 per cent. of the aggregate amount of local rates ; and real property *other than land* bore 64·7 per cent.   Now, dividing £16,727,000, the total Local Taxation, in the ratio of 35·3 to 64·7, it follows that the incidence is

£5,911,000 upon landed property,
and £10,816,000 upon real property other than land ;

but three-fourths of the tax upon land is paid by the owner, and one-half of the tax upon real property other than land is paid by the owner.   Hence

£4,433,000 is paid by *owners* of *land*,
and £5,408,000 is paid by *owners* of real property *other than land.*

Making £9,841,000, the total amount paid by the *owners* of real property.

Also, £1,478,000 is paid by *occupiers* of *land*,
and £5,408,000 is paid by *occupiers* of real property *other than land*.

Making £6,886,000, the total amount paid by the *occupiers* of real property, both land and otherwise.

But part of the sum total of £5,408,000 paid by *occupiers* of real property *other than land* will fall upon the manual labour classes. Mr. Dudley Baxter gives* £2,000,000 as the amount of rates paid by these classes in the *United Kingdom* upon an income of £325,000,000 : but the income of the manual labour classes in England and Wales is† £255,000,000, or thereabouts. We may therefore estimate that £1,569,000 will approximately be the amount of rates paid by these classes. Summarising the above results, we have :—

£9,841,000, the amount of Local Taxation falling upon *owners* of real property who are assessed under Schedule A.

£1,478,000, the amount falling upon *occupiers* of *land* whose profits are assessed to Income-tax under Schedule B.

£3,839,000 will fall upon *occupiers* of real property *other than land* whose incomes are assessed under Schedules C, D, E.

and £1,569,000 will fall upon the manual labour classes, and be paid out of their earnings.

In order to understand clearly the incidence of the aggregate Imperial and Local Taxation, let us consider the community to be divided into four classes :—

CLASS I.—Owners of real property, whose incomes correspond to those assessed to Income-tax under Schedule A.

CLASS II.—Occupiers of land, whose incomes correspond to those assessed under Schedule B.

CLASS III.—Occupiers of real property other than land, whose incomes are not derived from manual labour, and correspond to those assessed under Schedules C, D, E.

CLASS IV.—Manual labour classes, whose incomes are not assessed to Income Tax.

In Table IX., the approximate incomes possessed by each of these four classes is given ; the final total being the same as that in Table VI.

* "Taxation of the United Kingdom," App. iv., p. 176.   † P. 36, *supra*.

TABLE IX.

Approximate Incomes of the Community of England and Wales classified.

	£	£
CLASS I.—Incomes derived from Real Property, viz.:—		
Income-tax* charged in 1867 on	128,061,000	
The £60 per ann. excused to incomes between £100 and £200 per ann.	4,200,000	
Incomes under £100 per annum not charged to Income-tax	25,400,000	
		157,661,000
CLASS II.—Incomes of Occupiers of Land, viz.:—		
Income-tax charged in 1867 on	14,381,000	
The £60 per ann. excused to incomes between £100 and £200 per ann.	500,000	
Incomes under £100 per annum not charged to Income-tax	2,800,000	
		17,681,000
CLASS III.—Incomes derived from other sources, not being Manual Labour, viz.:—		
Income-tax charged in 1867 on	159,852,000	
The £60 per ann. excused to incomes between £100 and £200 per ann.	5,300,000	
Incomes under £100 per annum not charged to Income-tax	31,800,000	
Unreturned Profits under Schedule D......	49,076,000	
		246,028,000
CLASS IV.—Incomes derived from Manual Labour......		254,729,000
Total......		£676,099,000

* This amount includes £27,515,000 transferred to Schedule D. See page 35, supra.

By means of the data at pages 40 and 41, and in Table IX., we are now enabled to calculate at what rate per cent. the incomes of these four classes of the community are charged—

> (1) to Imperial Taxation ;
> (2) to Local Taxation;
> and (3) to the Aggregate Taxation of the country, by adding (1) and (2) together.

It should be noted here that the *Imperial Taxation* is shared by Class II. conjointly with Class III., the capital invested by the *occupier* of land being subject to the same imposts as property *other than land*. The per centage must, therefore, be the same in each case, and must be calculated on the joint incomes of Classes I. and II.—viz., a tax of £7,073,000 on an income of £263,709,000.

The results of these calculations are given in Table X. A comparison can then be instituted between the burdens borne by each class.

TABLE X.

Rates per cent. at which the Incomes of the four classes are charged to Imperial, Local, and the Aggregate Taxation.

CLASS I. — Charged to Imperial Taxation at 4 per cent.
        ,,   Local   ,,   ,, 6·2 ,,
        ,,   Aggregate ,,   ,, 10·2 ,,

CLASS II. — Charged to Imperial Taxation at 2·7 per cent.
        ,,   Local   ,,   ,, 8·3 ,,
        ,,   Aggregate ,,   ,, 11   ,,

CLASS III.—Charged to Imperial Taxation at 2·7 per cent.
        ,,   Local   ,,   ,, 1·5 ,,
        ,,   Aggregate ,,   ,, 4·2

CLASS IV.—Charged to Imperial Taxation   Nil.
        ,,   Local   ,,   at ·6 per cent.
        ,,   Aggregate ,,   ,, ·6   ,,

Here a great inequality of taxation becomes evident at a glance; and it must be remembered that the per centage in Table X. is calculated on the *total* incomes of the four classes: but Income-tax which is paid by Classes I., II., and III. is levied upon an income of £302,295,000* *only*, whilst the aggregate income of these three classes is £421,370,000. Hence the per-centage actually paid is rather higher than that given in Table X. It is necessary to calculate the per centage thus, because the incomes which are exempt from Income-tax are not exempt from other taxation.

Now, with the exceptions already mentioned of incomes under £100 per annum, and the exemption allowed on £60 to all incomes between £100 and £200 per annum, the Twelfth Report of the Commissioners of Inland Revenue declares, that " on lands and houses, on dividends and on salaries, and on pensions of public officers, the (income) tax is levied nearly to the uttermost farthing which is due" : that is, the incomes in Classes I. and II., and those in Class III., derived from dividends, salaries, and pensions, contribute their fair quota to the Income-tax; but the remainder of the incomes of Class III. (corresponding to the incomes assessed to Income-tax under Schedule D) evades the Income-tax on about £49,076,000,† as has been calculated above; and it is to be noted that these are the incomes of professional, mercantile, and trading communities. As Mr. Lowe describes it :—

> " Schedule D ‡ depends on the conscience of the tax-payer, who often, it is to be feared, returns hundreds instead of thousands, and who is certain to decide any question, that he can persuade himself to think doubtful, in his own favour."

Mr. Lowe's fears are fully justified by the experience of the In-land Revenue Commissioners. In one case, quoted in the Report,§ a person returned his income at £400 per annum, but, as soon as he began to expect that his premises would be required by the Metropolitan Board of Works, his return was increased to £1000. In another case, " on proceedings being taken, the defendants attempted to justify themselves by stating that 'their returns bore fully as large a proportion to their actual income as the

* Table VI.   † Page 37, *supra.*
‡ Draft Report to Income-tax Commissioners, 1861.
§ Twelfth Report, pp. 19—21.

returns made by their competitors and others in the trade,' and
that to have made true returns 'would have been in effect to
penalize themselves.' " This systematic fraud, moreover, is not
confined to any particular class, trade, or profession. The Commissioners found it prevailing amongst legal practitioners, public
companies, firms of world-wide reputation, and in every variety
of trade, and they estimate that in the United Kingdom the duty
is evaded on no less a sum than £57,254,997 ; and, "at the rate of
6d. in the pound, this would add to the revenue £1,431,374,
about the produce of a penny on the whole Income-tax." And
not only do the professional, mercantile, and trading communities
evade the tax due to Her Majesty's revenue on this large sum,
but they, together with others whose incomes are included in
Class III., only contribute incidentally to the Local Taxation of
the country, from the fact that they are obliged to dwell in houses,
and carry on their business and trade in offices, factories, and
shops. They pay only at the rate of 1·5 per cent.* on their
incomes ; and this, compared with the 6·2 and 8·3 per cent. paid
by Classes I. and II., is almost an exemption.

In his financial statement in 1853, Mr. Gladstone remarked
that " The exemption of one man means the taxation of another ;"
and again, on the 25th of June, 1869, he said :—

> " Exemption is the imposition of taxes upon others. An
> exemption is a concealed and latent grant, which men make
> without knowing it, and which hides the real state of things
> —the imposing of taxes upon others. It would be a most
> important amendment to introduce into the whole law of
> exemption from taxation, that there should be no such
> thing, except as a public grant."†

The owners of property, therefore, in Class III., have practically
a public grant at the expense of Classes I., II., and IV., a grant
which may be measured by the amount which they ought to
contribute as their fair proportion of the Local Taxation. And,
over and above this, the professional, mercantile, and trading
communities obtain, at the expense of the rest of the payers of
Income-tax, a grant of the immense sum by which they annually
defraud the revenue, whether altogether wilfully or not, does not
enter into the consideration of the matter in hand.

* Table X.

† Speech in the Debate on "Sunday and Ragged Schools Rating Exemption
Act," 1869.

CHAPTER IV

IT is often asserted that ratepayers have no real grievance to complain of, for that rates are no taxation at all, but a rent-charge on real property reserved to the State; that they never belonged to the purchaser, who, in consequence of their existence, paid less purchase-money than he otherwise would have done. Now, in the year 1776 the total amount of Local Taxation was £1,720,000, in 1868 it was £16,727,000, that is, in rather more than 80 years this impost has increased nine-fold. Can it be justly said that property was bought 80 years ago subject to the present charge, as a rent reserved to the State, and that the owner is not taxed? Is it not the more reasonable view of the matter that, as a purchaser acquires an estate subject to any new taxes the State may see fit to impose, so also he may fairly expect to have some of his old burdens removed from time to time; and it is right for him to try to get these old burdens removed or modified, when it is clear that they have become unjust and unequal in their action.

Mr. Dudley Baxter reduces the theory that rates are a reserved rent-charge to an arithmetical absurdity. The following argument is taken from his book on the "Taxation of the United Kingdom," the statistics for England and Wales being substituted for those given by Mr. Baxter.* It follows as a logical consequence of this theory, that the owner, being really not taxed by these rates, ought to be taxed again on his net income.

We have seen that the gross rental assessed to Local Taxation is £118,334,000,† and that the local rates amount to £16,727,000, and we have already shown that £9,841,000‡ comes out of the pockets of owners of lands and houses. Then, if the

* "Taxation of the United Kingdom," pp. 51—55.
† Tables II. and III.
‡ Page 40, *supra*.

theory under discussion is correct, the owners of this property, worth a rental of 118 millions, are not taxed in one farthing of the £9,841,000 by which their rents are diminished, but this large amount is a rent-charge belonging to the State, and with which they have nothing to do. It follows necessarily that, in justice to the other tax-payers, the owners ought to be taxed again to make up their full quota of taxation. Suppose, for the sake of argument, that the deficiency below this quota is 7 per cent. on £118,334,000 which would be £8,283,000, then this additional sum ought at once to be imposed on owners and their successors, and levied, as all taxes on property must, to be effectual, "at the source," *i.e.*, on the property itself. The gross amount payable to the State will thus become £18,124,000, in respect of £118,334,000 of rental.

But changes of property are continually occurring, both by death and sales. Every heir would inherit subject to the increased taxation, which would, therefore, on the reasoning of the theory, constitute a rent-charge due to the State. Every purchaser would deduct the whole outgoings from the price, and take care to secure a net income at 3 per cent. on his purchase money. Hence, after a certain lapse of time, when these changes have become universal, the old state of things recurs. The owners have bought or inherited, subject to the £18,124,000 rent-charge; and by the theory must be held to be unaffected by it. Not a penny of the £18,124,000, if the theory be correct, can be held to be their taxation; so that we must tax them again in another 7 per cent. on the net rental, so making up a gross assessment of £27,407,000 on the gross rental of £118,334,000.

But no sooner has this been done than the same causes begin to operate, and the same circle to recur again and again, until it is demonstrable by the strictest rules of logic—assuming the theory to be correct, and giving time for sufficient changes of property—that in the course of successive generations the owners may pay £109,237,000 out of the £118,334,000 in local taxes, and yet by the theory be perfectly untaxed, and require taxing again on their £9,097,000 of net income.

Mr. Baxter goes on to point out that "the theory con- Fallacies in tains three errors or fallacies which lead to this absurd this theory. conclusion. The first is a fallacy as to the principle of in-

heritance. By the English laws, a man is allowed to hand
down his money or land to his children with as complete
proprietorship as he himself enjoyed it, so that the ownership of the children is the same as that of the father, and
they cannot lose the reversion to the portion necessary to
pay the tax. It remains always a tax, continuing during
the will of the nation, and not a rent-charge which would be
the perpetual property of the State.

" The second fallacy is the assumption that purchasers
always buy with deduction of the taxes, and so obtain a
clear income on their purchase-money. This is the object at
which they aim, but every purchaser knows how often he
fails in obtaining it. Rates have also a tendency to increase, and to form a fresh burden on the property; and
fresh capital is invested at every change of ownership,
and during most ownerships, in improving the land and
buildings.

" The third fallacy consists in the forgetfulness of the
theorist, that purchase-money must come from somewhere,
and must itself have been subject to previous taxation. It
may have come from the sale of another landed estate or
houses, in which case it must have been realized at a loss,
which balances the deductions on the purchase. It may
have come from personal property; in which case it was
subject to Income-tax and probate and legacy duty, and was
diminished accordingly. Or it may have been savings from
income; in which case, according to our theorists, it has
been more heavily taxed in its acquirement than either of
the preceding properties. So that in every case the purchaser is merely exchanging one kind of taxation for another,
when he buys property; and the new taxes are as really
taxation as the old.

" Hence taxes on property, of however long standing,
must be counted as *bonâ-fide* taxation of the owners, just as
much as if they were taxes on income or expenditure."

Real property
has not
increased in
value so much
as other
property.

Again, it is confidently asserted that the value of real property
has increased more rapidly than the Local Taxation, and, therefore,
that the payment is less of a hardship now than formerly. Part
of this is only an *apparent* increase in value, because the assess-

ments are now more accurately made than formerly. Much, also, of the actual increase is due to the energy and enterprise of owners and occupiers, who have invested capital in improvements, which they might have employed otherwise, so that it should not be subject to the rates. But is the increased value of real property any reason for perpetuating an injustice? Has not the value of other kinds of property increased in a greater ratio than that of real property? Mr. Purdy calculates that, during the fifty years between 1815 and 1865,* whilst land rental increased 36 per cent., the profits of trades and professions increased 212 per cent. But it is now very generally allowed that gold has depreciated in value since the Californian and Australian gold discoveries in 1848 and 1850. Mr. Jevons,† in 1863, estimated this depreciation at 15 per cent.; so that, even if there has been no further depreciation since 1863, it would appear that rental has only increased 21 per cent. as against 197 per cent. increase of the profits of trades and professions; and it should be noted that, in Mr. Purdy's calculation, no allowance is made for the present more accurate valuation of real property, or for the unreturned profits of trades and professions, before alluded to, which would have the effect of lowering the per centage of increase of the former and raising that of the latter.

Mr. Mill‡ has a strange theory on the subject of the increase of value in land. He asserts—

> " That land is an exception to the ordinary rule of equality of taxation, because, with the increase of population, it spontaneously increases in value without any exertion or sacrifice on the part of the owners, but with complete passiveness on their part; so that it would be no violation of the principles on which private property is grounded, if the State should appropriate this increase of wealth, or part of it, as it arises, instead of allowing it to become an unearned appendage to the riches of a particular class."

If this theory be correct, then, in all equity, it must be applied to the owners of every kind of property. The State would have

---

* Journal of Stat. Soc., vol. xxxii., pt. iii., p. 318.
† See a Pamphlet published by Messrs. Stanford, Charing Cross, 1863.
‡ " Political Economy," Book v., c. ii., s. 5.

a right to appropriate any part of a merchant's profits which was unearned. If, after a merchant had laid in a stock of goods, the prices rose, the State ought to appropriate the increased value, or part of it, because the increase is not due to any "exertion" on the part of the merchant, but has arisen "with complete passiveness" on his part; but land and houses are frequently bought by speculators, who give a high price in the hope of an increase in their value. Here, as in the case of merchants, there is a risk that they may have miscalculated, and that the value should fall instead of rise. Moreover, if the State may appropriate the "spontaneous increase" in value of property, it must also ensure the owner against decrease, and all stimulus to industry and improvement in every line would thereby be removed, and the effect would be a speedy demoralization of the community. Mr. Dudley Baxter says* that—

> "Stripped to its kernel Mr. Mill's theory is simply this, that landowners are only entitled in strictness to a rent-charge upon their estates, and that the improving interest and its disposal is the property and prerogative of the State. But this is a clause out of a totally different creed as to the rights of property, and a different policy from those which have formed the foundation of the laws of England."

The growth of pauperism commensurate with the increase of commercial wealth.

It has already been shown† that the great increase of wealth during the last fifty years has been chiefly commercial and professional; it is also an ascertained fact that the immense growth of pauperism in the country has been commensurate with this increase. We do not say that the whole of the pauperism is to be laid at the door of commerce; but a great proportion is certainly due to failures, commercial panics, and dishonest speculations. Failures and panics cannot always be foreseen and avoided; but they entail a vast amount of misery and distress on the working population. In every manufacture there is a tendency for supply to outrun the demand for consumption. This is a necessary consequence of the activity of trade. When this happens there is a glut in that particular manufacture, and the manufacturer reduces the number of his work-people. Again, the supply of raw material necessary for carrying on a manufac-

---

* "Taxation of United Kingdom," ch. xi., p. 57.   † P. 40, *supra.*

ture may fail. No one can have forgotten how the failure of the cotton supply, during the late American civil war, affected the cotton manufactures in Lancashire. Thousands upon thousands of operatives were thrown out of work, and, had it not been for the noble liberality of those who came forward voluntarily to help them, the distress would have been still more severely felt. Dishonest speculation, too, contributes its quota of the misery. A failure ensues, and there is no resource for those who were employed but to come upon the rates, paid by the occupiers of the neighbouring land and houses, for support. Many of them, moreover, cannot turn their hands to any other work than that to which they have been accustomed.

Professor Leone Levi computes that, on the average, the labouring classes are out of work only four weeks in the fifty-two; Mr. Dudley Baxter, however, thinks the state of affairs far different. And, indeed, no one can see the numbers of people who are constantly seeking for employment, and are living in a state of semi-starvation, without believing that Mr. Baxter is more likely to be right, when he says that* 20 per cent. ought to be deducted from the nominal full-time wages. Mr. Baxter made this computation in 1868; but it would seem that even this deduction is not sufficient for the present time, so much has the demand for labour fallen off. Multitudes, even of skilled labourers, have been discharged from our dockyards and manufactories, who can find no employment elsewhere; but such is their innate respectability and love of independence, that numbers will pawn their necessary clothing, and endure even to starvation point, rather than lose their self-respect by applying for relief. The distress and suffering to be seen daily amongst these artisans is hardly conceivable.

It would be very instructive if the Poor Law Board would issue a return giving the proportional numbers of those relieved, in the various divisions and Unions of England and Wales, to each of the four classes of occupation—domestic, commercial, agricultural, and industrial. At the census of 1861, out of a total of 10,983,558† of persons aged 20 years and upwards, the agricultural population numbered 1,605,503, or 14·6 per cent.; and the industrial or artisan class numbered 3,746,788, or 34·1

* "National Income," ch. iv., p. 47.
† Twenty-first Report of the Poor Law Board. App. C. No. 31, p. 244.

per cent. Is it just that land, tithes, and houses should be called upon to support the trade-made poor ? When we consider the enormous incomes that are acquired, and the vast amount of capital that is amassed by means of the labour of these very poor, is it equitable that those who benefit by their labour should contribute nothing to their support ?

Non-liability of fundholders to taxation. It is argued that the State has no right to tax income derived from the funds ; and to prove this, the original Act* of 1692 is quoted. Under this Act a million was raised by Life Annuities, and as each annuity fell in it was to be divided amongst the others, until there were only seven survivors; after that time the public were to gain. The interest was to be 10 per cent. till the year 1700; and after that year 7 per cent. The Act provided that money lent "shall not be charged or chargeable with any rates, duties, or impositions whatever." All subsequent Acts for borrowing money have words to the like effect. It is contended, therefore, that the State is bound by law and honour to maintain the exemption of the owners of funded property from Local Taxation. Those who argue this forget that the State already levies Income-tax under Schedule C from these ; and that this Income-tax increases or diminishes according to the necessities of the national exchequer. Besides, no one proposes to rate the property—i.e., the principal—in the funds, but only the income derived therefrom ; and this would no more be a breach of faith than is the Income-tax for Imperial purposes. The fundholder enjoys the interest of his investment in security and comfort, and there is no reason why he should expect the owners of real property to pay for his advantages. In the reign of William and Mary there was not this security. It was by no means impossible that there should be a revolution restoring the Stuarts ; and then all who had advanced money to the government of William would have lost both principal and interest.

Real property enjoys no special privileges. It cannot be said that real property is now in possession of any exclusive privileges which would justify its bearing so large a share of the national burdens. By the abolition of the shilling duty on imported corn the last rag of protection has been torn away. It is allowed that the possession of property in land gives dignity to the possessor, and that the occupation of farming is pleasant and health-giving ; and therefore that incomes from

* 4th and 5th William and Mary, c. 3., s. 26.

these sources should bear a somewhat larger amount of taxation
in the aggregate than incomes from personal property. Mr.
Baxter is of opinion that these incomes should pay a per centage
of taxes one-fifth higher than incomes derived from personalty.
Again, incomes derived from personal property should be taxed
at a higher rate than incomes that are called industrial, which
are precarious in their nature. All professions and appoint-
ments which are for life, or of which the income is fluctuating,
ought to pay less than incomes from personal property. Mr.
Mill considers that one-fourth of these fluctuating or industrial
incomes should be exempt from taxation.

> "A man with £500 a year from business would consider
> his family well provided for at his death by an insurance or
> savings producing £250 a year—that is to say, by a capital
> of £6000. This amount, insured on a good life, and com-
> mencing at 20 years of age, will cost in premiums about
> £125 a year, or one-fourth of his income. Savings (which
> avoid the stamp-duty, expenses, and profit of insurance com-
> pany) ought, on an average length of life, to produce the
> same capital from a less annual sum. Hence, one-fourth is
> a fair allowance of exemption for an industrial income."

Now, in levying a single tax, it is impossible to adjust it in
this manner to the different classes of income; but the aggregate
amount paid by each ought to approximate to this proportion,
in order that the burden of taxation may be fairly borne. But
it has been shown in Table X. that

CLASS I.—Income from real property pays 10·2 per cent.
CLASS II.— ,, of occupiers of land ,, 11·0 ,, ,,
CLASS III.— ,, from other sources ,, 4·2 ,, ,,

And Class III. comprises owners of incomes from personal property, and of industrial incomes; and it is probable that the
former pay 5·4 per cent., and the latter 3 per cent.

Thus, the per centage on the incomes of the owners of land
and houses is double, and that of occupiers of land nearly 1 per
cent. more than double that paid by incomes from realized pro-

perty; whilst industrial incomes are charged with less than one-third the taxation that is borne by Classes I. and II.

When, therefore, it is asserted that incomes from real property do not bear a fair proportion of taxation, because real property is exempt from probate-duty, it may be confidently answered that the very reverse is the true statement of the case; for that real property bears a far greater proportion of the aggregate taxation of the country than is due. And this may be indisputably proved by statistics.

As Mr. Disraeli* said in 1851 :—

> "The Government interferes with no other property or interest as it does with the landed (or real property). Suppose the same laws applied to manufacturers. What speeches! what leagues we should have!"

* "Times," Feb. 11th, 1851.

CHAPTER V.

THE objects, to which the proceeds of Local Taxation are applied, may be divided into two groups:—

First.—Those which are *national*.
Second.—Those which are *purely local*.

In the first group would be placed the tax which is called Poor-rate, every item of which is expended on objects more or less national in their character, and for the welfare of the public generally. The same may be said of the amount levied for County, Hundred, Borough, or Police Rates, in those cases where these are not paid out of the Poor-rate. The taxes in this group amount to £11,361,745.

Can it be denied that all classes of the community derive protection for their property and safety for their persons through the existence and operation of the Poor-laws, whether they are owners or occupiers, manufacturers, merchants, or tradesmen? Sir George Cornewall Lewis, in his evidence before the Committee of the House of Lords,* gave his opinion very clearly in answer to the questions asked him:—

" Q. 2378. The object of my question was rather to elicit your opinion upon the question, whether that general system of liability which attaches to all realized property to maintain the poor of the country, would attach equally to annual profits?—Yes; I see no reason why annual profits should not be as much taxed as the produce of realized property, if a national Income-tax were in question.

" 2379. You think that a person deriving £1000 a year from his professional business, or from any annual source, is as reasonably, and in justice equally subject to maintain the

* Committee of the House of Lords on Parochial Assessments, 1850.

poor as the owner of realized property is?—That involves the question of a graduated Income-tax; my own opinion is unfavourable to a graduated Income-tax, as I wish to see all persons contribute equally from their means, whether it be realized property, or whether it be profits of trade or professions. I am quite aware that it is an opinion which is not generally acquiesced in, and that very specious arguments may be adduced on the other side.

"2380. I wish to draw your attention to a principle which seems different from the principle of a graduated Income-tax. The first obligation attaching to all existing property is generally admitted to be the obligation of maintaining the existence of all persons in the country; the object of my question is, to ascertain your opinion as to whether that obligation attaches upon the same grounds, and upon the same principle, to profits which people are making by individual exertions, as to realized property, which they actually possess?—Yes; I see no reason for making any distinction. If I were imposing a national Income-tax, to be applied to the relief of the poor, I should impose it according to the same rate upon the profits of trade, upon professions, and upon the produce of realized property.

"2381. You think the claim of the poor to the right of maintenance attaches with the same strength to profits which an individual is making by his personal annual exertions, as it does to realized property?—Yes.

"2382. The realization of those profits is the result of the civilized institutions of the country?—Yes. In order to exercise industry with advantage, it is necessary that there should be security of property. It is necessary that there should be good communications. It is necessary that the insurance of property which is paid by the relief of the poor (for it may be considered as a species of insurance) should fall also upon that class of persons.

"2383. Do you not consider that the existence of the Poor Law in this country is a great protection to property? —I entertain no doubt whatever that a well-managed Poor Law, not suffered to excite unreasonable expectations, but carefully applied to the relief of the most pressing forms of destitution, must be considered as a very material addition to the security of our institutions.

"2384. Not of property only, but of industry also?— Yes; it is difficult to distinguish between industry and property. No doubt it is a material security to both."

But, again, are not all classes equally concerned in the efficiency of the Police? Is not the small-pox as terrible to the merchant as to the yeoman? Why should real property be charged with nearly the whole cost of maintaining coroners and militia storehouses? Why should coal mines contribute to the support of the poor, whilst metallic mines are exempt? Why should a farmer pay for the inspection of a tradesman's weights and measures?

In the second group of objects, which are purely local in their nature, would be placed Highway Rates, Lighting, and Watching Rates, Public Health Rates, etc., and they amount to £5,365,429. Now these rates though expended on local objects, yet are for the welfare of the whole community residing in the district where they are levied. The waggons of the manufacturer cause as much wear and tear to the highways as those of the farmer. The use of carriages is not confined to the owners of real property.

We have[*] shown above that the Act of the 43rd of Elizabeth contemplated that all should contribute according to their ability; but granting, for argument's sake, that real property was intended by that Act, because it was then nearly the whole wealth of the country; will any one urge that this state of things is to exist always, and that the changed circumstances of the national wealth do not justify a corresponding change in the taxation? Will it be said that the State, finding the existing system unjust and unequal, has no right to alter it. In Queen Elizabeth's time the trade of the country was in its infancy, and the moneyed interest was unknown. It remained for the versatile and vigorous mind of Montague to devise the scheme, which has since developed into the largest national debt ever known. It was under his auspices that the Bank of England was established, the prosperity of which is bound up with the prosperity of the country. In these days when the commercial, the manufacturing, and the moneyed interest has increased so enormously, it is time

* Page 9, *supra.*

that they should bear their share of a burden which it is a public duty to sustain.

It must be carefully borne in mind that this is a question affecting ratepayers generally, whether residing in towns or in the country. It is not a matter which is interesting only to the landowner and farmer. It is a grievance that concerns the town populations also; and, contrary to one of the first principles of taxation, the burden presses most on those who have small incomes; namely, upon the struggling tradesman as compared with the opulent banker, upon the mechanic, or factory operative as compared with his employer.

Those who profess to believe that there is no unfairness in the present system of Local Taxation, are continually attempting to raise a false issue. They would persuade us, that the advocates of a reform are setting class against class; that the agricultural interest is trying to throw the load upon the shoulders of the town population; that the landlords and owners are striving to gain a benefit at the expense of the occupiers. Enough has been advanced to show that there are no grounds for these charges. It is the duty of all who profess to be friends of the working-man, and would wish to see him living in a better and more comfortable dwelling, and, where possible, with a plot of ground for cultivation in his leisure hours, to labour to lighten his burdens. It is the duty of all, who have regard for the broad principles of morality and justice, to endeavour to obtain a redistribution of the burden, well nigh intolerable in its present incidence, so that it may be placed upon a fair and equitable basis.

CHAPTER VI.

THE consideration of the way in which these grievances are to be Various proposals of reform. reformed does not, properly speaking, belong to an essay like the present; but it may not be out of place to glance at some of the suggestions that have been offered, and to attempt to show how far they are practicable.

It has been proposed that a grant-in-aid from the Consoli- Grant from Consolidated Fund. dated Fund would meet the difficulties of the case; but such a grant would not remove the injustice of the practice by which real property alone is rated. The burden of the rates would, it is true, be lightened; but the rates would still be levied on one class of property, and this is the anomaly which requires to be reformed. Moreover, such a grant would be a compromise which would supplement one injustice by another. The community of the United Kingdom contribute to the Consolidated Fund, and it would not be just to require the taxpayers of Scotland and Ireland to give towards the relief of the poor of England and Wales.

Much more practicable is the proposal that the present A national rate on the basis of the Income-tax assessment. system of rates should be abolished, and a national rate be levied on the basis of the Income-tax assessment; but it is urged against this scheme that the funds would then be administered with reckless extravagance; that, under the present system, the guardians of each union are personally interested in an economical expenditure, and that the ratepayers would call them to account at the first instance of any disregard of economy; but that this wholesome check would be at once removed when the guardians could draw upon a national fund, and, in fact, that each union would then strive to grasp as large a share of this fund as it could induce the authorities to grant. Without any doubt there is a great deal of truth in this argument, and, if one check be removed, it certainly becomes necessary to obtain some other guarantee for economy. Would not such a guarantee be

obtained by the adoption of a plan somewhat similar to that
Lord Malmesbury's Proposal in 1850. suggested by Lord Malmesbury in 1850—namely, that a limit should be fixed to the demands of each union district on the proposed national fund? This limit might be determined by taking the average expenditure of a certain number of years, and making a grant to that amount, holding the guardians responsible for all they expended in excess of such grant; and this rule should never be relaxed, except under the most pressing circumstances, such, for instance, as the late distress in Lancashire. The necessity for such departure from the rule ought to be certified, after strict investigation, by authorities having no immediate or personal interest in the district. A Special Board, appointed by the Poor Law Board, consisting of Poor Law Inspectors, would answer the purpose, without any great extra expense being incurred. Such a system might with advantage be applied to taxation in aid of relief to the poor. Without any doubt the present system of local management would have to be modified in some degree, but all are agreed that the principle must be retained, it being especially dear to the Anglo-Saxon mind, which has an instinctive dread of centralization. It cannot, however, be expected that any government should hand over funds to local authorities without retaining in their hands the right of insisting upon a proper and economical use being made of their grants. Some have proposed that the Poor Law Inspec-

Poor Law Inspectors to be *ex officio* Chairmen of Board of Guardians. tors should be *ex officio* Chairmen of Boards of Guardians, thus combining local management with a direct supervision by the agents of the central authorities. Now, it would naturally be expected that a proposal for the equalization of rates throughout the country would, at all events, meet with the approval of those unions where the rates would be reduced considerably, even if some amount of local consequence and fancied dignity had to be resigned by the guardians; but it does not follow that such would be the case. A writer in the " Quarterly Review "* very forcibly points out the want of public spirit in local administration.

He points to " Our whole system of *Municipal Adminis-tration*, with its inextricable confusion, and its astounding and costly inefficiency—imbued throughout with the

* " Quarterly Review," No. 253, July, 1869, p. 46.

'vestry' spirit, guided everywhere by the 'vestry' mind.
Men elected by household suffrage, often practically by the
lowest householders under the influence of the corruptest
motives, for the most part immersed in their own private
businesses, usually half-educated and always quite untrained
in administrative functions, are entrusted with the management of large funds, and the direction of the most important
social and civic undertakings, such as police, lighting, paving,
draining, scavenging, etc., and discharge them,—as we see.
Grocers, and publicans, and speculative builders, or the
nominees of less enlightened classes still, determine what
rates shall be levied, and how they shall be expended; ap-
point amateur surveyors of roads, perfunctory inspectors of
nuisances, commissioners or boards of public works; em-
ploying fragments of their time, and the spare portions of
'what they are pleased to call their mind,' on objects which
might well task the full powers of the best professional
capacities. In this enormous overgrown metropolis, the evils
of this inappropriate system are even more salient than elsewhere, and, while more manifest and more monstrous, are
more difficult to deal with ; and we are virtually managing
and governing the greatest city, or congeries of cities, in the
world, through the antiquated machinery of a dozen vestries,
aided by half a dozen boards improvised for special services,
but often, like the vestries themselves, consisting of untrained functionaries. Yet so deeply is the notion of vestry
rule ingrained in the middle-class English mind, that, keenly
as we all feel the discredit and discomfort of this state of
things, it seems as if no Government could summon up the
combined strength, courage, and capacity to grapple with
the mischief, and apply a remedy."

Mr. Goschen, in a speech on the Metropolitan Poor Law
Amendment Bill, mentioned a fact indicative of the sort of petty
motives and narrow views which often govern Boards of Guardians.
Speaking of the amalgamation of unions, he said :—

"In this matter there was rather delicate ground for
him to touch upon, but he felt it his duty to do so. In the
City of London there were three unions—the City of London

proper, with rateable property valued at £1,800,000; and the
West London and the East London, each of which had rateable property valued at £200,000. In the first-named of
these unions the rate was only 7d. in the pound ; in each of
the two others it was 3s. The Poor Law Board had asked
the guardians of the two latter unions whether they would
consent to their own dissolution, in order that they might
be united to the rich union, the City of London proper,
whereby their rates would be reduced from 3s. to 11d. or 1s.
He had not received an answer to that question; but from
the proceedings of the West London Union he perceived
that the guardians were much dissatisfied with the proposal.
Indeed, it would appear from their debate that there was no
chance of their consenting to it. He had imagined that the
union of the City of London proper might be opposed to his
proposal; but he had not supposed that the poorer unions
would object to a scheme which would reduce their rate so
considerably."

It is, however, to be hoped, that those ratepayers who in
many places are paying as much as 5s., 6s., and even 7s. in the
pound,* will see the advantage of introducing a system by which
they would, at the very highest calculation, have to pay 1s. This
result may be obtained by extending the area of Local Taxation
for objects of a national character to the wider basis of the
Income-tax assessment, with some modifications. Numbers o
those who are assessed under Schedule D would, no doubt, con-
trive to evade the payment; for it is not to be expected that
those who make a practice of defrauding Her Majesty's revenue
by understating their incomes, would cease to do so when taxed
for other purposes under the proposed system. The exemption
of a certain amount of income might be allowed; perhaps £50
would be a fair maximum. It will be allowed that this is not
more than sufficient to provide its owner with the mere neces-
saries of life, especially if he has a family, as is the case with
many of the working classes, whose incomes on the average do
not reach £60 a year. The maximum amount to be exempted,
being fixed, should be deducted from every income. Thus the
possessor of an income of £50 per annum would not be rated, the

* See Table IV., page 18.

possessor of an income of £100 per annum would be rated on £50. Mr. Mill originally enunciated this principle of obviating the inequality in the Income-tax, by which the possessor of an income of £99 would escape taxation; but the possessor of an income of £100 would pay the ordinary per centage. Mr. Gladstone adopted this principle in a modified form in his Budget of 1863. And all incomes below £100 per annum are exempt: whilst the possessors of incomes between £100 and £200 per annum are allowed to deduct £60, and pay Income-tax on the remainder.

With regard to the objection, that a national fund adminis- *The principle that a national fund may be administered by local authorities has been admitted.* tered by local authorities would necessarily lead to great extravagance, it may be pointed out that Mr. Goschen's Metropolitan Poor Act (1867) Amendment Bill has already admitted the principle, without any guarantee or check against unlimited expenditure by particular unions of general funds contributed by the unions of the Metropolis. By this Bill, any excess of expenditure above a specified rate in the pound is to be repaid to the guardians of any union in the Metropolis out of the Metropolis Common Poor Fund. Now, if this principle is applicable to the Metropolis, why should it not be extended to the country generally? There is, moreover, great reason to believe that, by the introduction of a uniform system of administration in England and Wales, a great saving would be effected, which at present is hardly possible, when each Board of Guardians has its own system.

It may not be amiss to direct attention to the system pursued *System in the U. S. of America.* in the United States of America. A correspondent of the "Journal of the Chamber of Agriculture"* writes, that in the United States "all municipal and state taxes are assessed on the entire property, real and personal, of every description, held by the inhabitants of towns and cities (that is, parishes). The municipal authority of each city or town (equivalent to our borough or parochial authority) first determines and fixes the amount of money to be raised for all branches of the public service—as, a certain sum for highways, a certain sum for the support of schools, a certain sum for the support of the poor, etc.—the estimates being based upon the experience of past years

---

* "Journal of Chamber of Agriculture," No. 25, March 9, 1869, p. 204.

as a guide to the probable amounts that may be required for the current year. After the full amount required for any city or town (parish) is determined, there is added to such sum the proportion of state and county taxes assessed on such city or town. Then this total contribution is assessed by the assessors of the city or town upon the real and personal property of the citizens. Each citizen is required by law to render to the assessors a full and accurate valuation of his entire property. He can be put on oath by the assessors; and, when there is reason to believe the valuation not correct, the assessors can change and amend it. Agricultural implements, the tools of mechanics up to a given value, and a given amount of household furniture for poor people, are exempt from taxation and attachment. Thus, Poor-rates and other taxes are assessed on the entire property of citizens, who are able to pay. When a person has property in one town or State where his home is not situated, that property is taxed in the town where it is located. Each State provides for the poor within its limits, if a settlement there has existed for the time required by law. If it can be shown that the settlement is in some other State, the poor needing relief are returned to the State where they have a right to claim a residence or support."

Conclusion. It is a feeling that has been increasing of late years, that a reform in the various matters that have been discussed is necessary to suit the altered requirements of the times; neither can the consideration of measures for lightening the burdens now pressing unduly upon real property be much longer postponed. It is a subject which may be discussed without the bitterness of a party contest; and it is only reasonable to hope that a Reformed House of Commons, which has not shrunk from the arduous task of attempting the pacification of Ireland, will not feel itself unwilling or unable to remove a grievance which presses most unjustly upon many of the most peaceable and law-abiding of Her Majesty's subjects.

F. BENTLEY AND CO., PRINTERS, LONDON.

www.ingramcontent.com/pod-product-compliance
Lightning Source LLC
Chambersburg PA
CBHW021523090426
42739CB00007B/752